I0467694

Employee Recognition

The KISS Theory

A simple straightforward approach to personal and professional development.

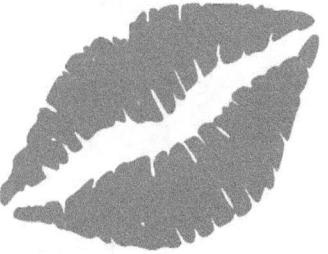

Jayne Finn

Copyright © 2015 by Jayne Finn
Copyright © 2015 by Global Courseware, Inc.

www.thekisstheory.com

All rights reserved. No part of this publication may be reproduced, distributed, or transmitted in any form or by any means, including photocopying, recording, or other electronic or mechanical methods, without the prior written permission of the publisher, except in the case of brief quotations embodied in critical reviews and certain other non-commercial uses permitted by copyright law. The material in this book is for educational purposes. Permission requests should be submitted to the publisher in writing at one of the addresses below:

73 Greentree Drive, Suite 68, Dover, Delaware 19904
United States of America

116 Provost Street, New Glasgow, Nova Scotia, B2H 2P4
Canada

ISBN – 13: 978-1522702764
ISBN – 10: 1522702768

Your value doesn't decrease based on someone's inability to see your worth.

Unknown

To the Reader

I've been fascinated with the KISS principle for several years now. What is this KISS principle that's got me so excited?

KISS principle

KISS stands for "Keep It Simple, Stupid" – a design principle the U.S. Navy developed in 1960. Aircraft engineer Kelly Johnson (1910-1990) has often been associated with the Kiss principle. It basically means a majority of systems work best if there is no complexity behind them. Therefore, when it comes to design, there should be no complexity involved.

You may have noticed the 1+1 does not equal two on the book cover. We are taught from preschool that 1+1=2 a simple equation. Other mathematical theories prove different that 1 +1 does not = 2. Personal development is presented as a complex process. Once it is broken down into simple steps there should not be complexity involved.

As a teacher and facilitator I have searched for way to develop a simpler way to approach personal and professional development. I have found it can start with a few moments a day of mindful thoughts and simple awareness of self and how we interact with others.

And, it was from this that the KISS theory came about. They're simple easy to read books that can provide insightful thoughts that can be used immediately. I have changed the "Keep It Simple Stupid" phrase, with "Keep It Strategically Simple." I certainly feel it gives a much better tone to get you to take action. Personal development begins with self-awareness; an awareness for us to improve and be a better version of who we are. When you reach the end of each chapter, you'll be greeted with practical illustrations, questions and a chance to write your thoughts down.

After all, I am a motivational quote enthusiast. And, as an adjunct instructor, I provide students with additional credits on tests if they memorize the quotes on the board. As an author, I issue you this challenge: memorize a quote or two for extra credit for your own self-discovery.

I am delighted to go on this journey with you.

Dedication and Acknowledgement

Dedicated to my husband, Terry Finn through personal sacrifice, and selflessness, bestowed the support and understanding without which this journey would not have been possible. I love you.

I also want to acknowledge our sons and daughter Todd, Tina, and Quentin whose personal development as adults have inspired me. My friend, Theresa Peaden who years ago encouraged me to pursue teaching and training (I thought she was crazy.) and provided me the opportunity to find my passion.

Simple Thoughts

"If you can't explain it to a six-year-old you don't understand it yourself."

Albert Einstein

"Genius is the ability to reduce the complicated to the simple."

C.W. Ceran

"We need to simplify life. Do you think grass thinks about who trod on it yesterday? No... It just continues to grow. And so should you. You cannot control who treads on you, but you do control your own growth. Don't ever let others inhibit you!"

Tony Curl

"Only those who have patience to do *simple* things perfectly ever acquire the skill to do difficult things easily."

James J. Corbett

"Life is really simple, but we insist on making it complicated."

Confucius

"Our life is frittered away by detail. Simplify, simplify."

Henry David Thoreau

"There is no greatness where there is not simplicity, goodness, and truth."

Leo Tolstoy

"Nature is pleased with simplicity. And nature is no dummy"

Isaac Newton

"If you will stay close to nature, to its simplicity, to the small things hardly noticeable, those things can unexpectedly become great and immeasurable."

Rainer Maria Rilke

"Nothing is more simple than greatness; indeed, to be simple is to be great."

Ralph Waldo Emerson

"I am not a genius; I am just curious. I ask many questions. and when the answer is simple, then God is answering."

Albert Einstein

"People often associate complexity with deeper meaning, when often after precious time has been lost, it is realized that simplicity is the key to everything."

Gary Hopkins

"To say more while saying less is the secret of being simple."

Dejan Stojanovic

"The truth is always simple. It's the mind that complicates it."

Joseph Rain

"My task is to simplify and then go deeper, making a commitment to what remains. That's what I've been after. To care and polish what remains till it glows and comes alive from loving care."

Sue Bender

"Human beings, viewed as behaving systems, are quite simple. The apparent complexity of our behavior over time is largely a reflection of the complexity of the environment in which we find ourselves."

Herbert A. Simon

"Simplicity is a kind of transparency in which subtle nuances can have outsize effects."

David Byrne

Wisdom is the highest strength; simplicity has intrinsic power."

Debasish Mridha M.D.

"Simplicity allows a measure of freedom which the complexities of modern life greedily consume freedom to think, to reflect, to create, to serve and be sincerely generous with our time and presence."

Mary Morrell

"It's the simplest things that can convey a message...."

Peter Cimino

"Here's to the moments when you realize the simple things are wonderful and enough."

Jill Badonsky

"That's been one of my mantras — focus and simplicity. Simple can be harder than complex: You have to work hard to get your thinking clean to make it simple. But it's worth it in the end because once you get there, you can move mountains. [BusinessWeek, May 25 1998]"

Steve Jobs

CONTENTS

Make it a habit to tell people thank you. To express your appreciation, sincerely and without the expectation of anything in return. Truly appreciate those around you, and you'll soon find many others around you. Truly appreciate life, and you'll find that you have more of it.

Ralph Marston

Preface

To a business, an employee recognition program is not a luxury, it is a necessity. With a well-built employee recognition program, companies can improve job retention, employee engagement, team work, reinforcing company values, and more. Employees are more likely to continue employment with a company if they feel they are appreciated. There are many different types of employee recognition programs, and all are beneficial to your employees.

Happiness does not come from doing easy work but from the afterglow of satisfaction that comes after the achievement of a difficult task that demanded our best.

Theodore Isaac Rubin

Chapter One:
The Many Types of Incentive

Like ice cream, there are many flavors of employee recognition programs. Being able to assess what program or programs are needed is essential to a company's success. Research shows that 79 percent of people who quit their jobs cite lack of appreciation as the main reason, and recent focus groups on appreciation found employees become disengaged when they don't feel appreciated. Employee recognition programs, can keep employees motivated, safe, happy, and invested in your business.

Safety Incentives

Safety incentive programs are programs designed to help maintain the safety goals of a company. These goals could be tailored to the company's needs. Reviewing the on-the-job accident statistics is generally a good place to start assessing if you need a safety incentive in place, and what for. According to OSHA, there are on average, more than 84 work related deaths per week or nearly 12 deaths every day. Nearly 3.0 million nonfatal workplace injuries and illnesses were reported in 2012. 18.9% of injuries reported in 2012 where back related. The most common, making up 24.7% of all reported injuries, are due to falls. As an employer you have a responsibility to keep your employees safe. An injured employee can cost the company immeasurable amounts of money. An effective safety program can save $4 to $6 for every $1 invested.

Years of Service

Most employees remember their hire date; it's the career equivalent of wedding anniversary. Just as we celebrate our wedding anniversary milestones, employers should strive to celebrate their employees' work anniversaries.

Employee job abandonment costs companies thousands of dollars. According to Webpronews, a study showed that it costs 30-50% of their annual salary to replace an entry-level employee, and 150% of the annual salary of a mid-level employee and up to 400% for specialized, high level employee. What contribute to the cost of job abandonment?

- Exit costs
- Recruiting
- Interviewing

- Hiring
- Orientation
- Training
- Lost productivity
- Temporary workers

Recognizing an employee's years of service is a simple way to express to your employees they are appreciated. Recognizing an employee and showing them that their time and effort matter is vital in retaining your prized employees.

Productivity

The old saying goes "Happy wife, Happy life". This saying can also be turned around to "Happy employees, Happy company." Employee recognition programs that focus on productivity help to encourage employees and increase production. These programs can be tailored to a specific department's function. Increasing productivity in each department increases the productivity of the company as a whole. It is vital to remember when setting your productivity goals to make them realistic. Offering a reward for a goal that is unattainable will not strengthen your company, but hinder it.

Attendance & Wellness Incentives

Attendance incentives are based only on attendance. A good way to utilize an attendance incentive is by adding it to a yearly review. An employee may feel motivated to go to work more often if they have a chance of obtaining a raise. Unscheduled absenteeism is a chronic problem for U.S. employers, conservatively costing $3,500 per hourly employee, and $2,500 per salaried employee per year. Keeping employees motivated to go to work is essential to a company's success.

Many companies are starting to realize that healthier employees mean lower insurance costs, and higher productivity. Wellness incentives are being used to help employees adopt and maintain a healthy lifestyle. Keeping those employees healthy means better attendance rates. An employee wellness incentive plan can come in many different forms:

- Rewarding employees for attending no-cost health education seminars
- Waiver of co-pay under a group health plan for preventive care
- Providing employees with free flu shots and required vaccinations

- Reimbursement of costs for participating in a smoking cessation program
- Reward for completing a health risk assessment
- Reimbursing workers for gym memberships
- Offering weight loss programs
- Providing free health coaching
- Offering insurance-premium discounts to those who meet health standards

A study conducted by Harvard University found wellness program returns to be about $3.27 per dollar spent in reduced medical costs and $2.73 per dollar spent in reduced absenteeism costs. Excessive employee absences can reduce productivity, lower morale, and increase rates of job turnover. Keeping your employees happy and healthy just makes 'cents'!

Practical Illustration

Jennifer has been at the same job for five years. When she first started, she was excited to go to work. She went in every day with a drive to go above and beyond. Jennifer's boss sees her as a good employee. She scores high on her yearly performance review, and is great at her job. Lately, Jennifer has lost the drive and excitement, and does just the minimum of her required work load. She is also late and absent more often these days. Jennifer has been feeling underappreciated and invisible to her company. She can't remember the last time she felt praised or encouraged. She has been considering applying for work at a competitor's company. Jennifer has heard from former co-workers that their work environment is geared more towards the employee than the bottom line.

Personal Journal - *What are two or three points you can take from this chapter to enhance your company's employee recognition experience?*

You can design and create, and build the most wonderful place in the world. But it takes people to make the dream a reality.

Walt Disney

Chapter Two:
Designing Employee Recognition Programs

Developing an employee recognition program can be a huge boost for employee engagement and satisfaction. Some studies have shown that recognition is listed highest in employee satisfaction. Employee recognition programs can promote the core values and beliefs of a company while building a more engaged employee base.

Purpose

First step is deciding what the purpose of your program is with goals. These goals should be clearly defined, and meaningful to your organization. You can start by asking yourself questions about the program, and what you hope to achieve. Utilize your team members when deciding the goals of your employee recognition program. Sometimes having a second opinion, or another prospective will shed light onto goals that you wouldn't have considered prior. Once you have defined your goals, you can decide what type of employee recognition program you need to implement in order to facilitate reaching that goal. You may also want to ask yourself these questions:

- What will the employees need to do be rewarded?

- What employee behaviors will the program reward?

- What employee achievements should be recognized?

- What end results are you looking for?

- What policies and practices will your recognition program highlight?

For example, you decide that you would like to have an incentive program that's goal is to decrease workplace accidents. Now that you have decided that your goal will be safety oriented, you can proceed in deciding the reward.

Safety incentive program: Setting the number of days without recordable accidents or number of months without lost-time injuries, if met, a reward is given.

The program should have objectives to guide when making decisions about the program.

These objectives can be referenced when determining the amount of time and money to dedicate to the program.

Jim Brintnall, author of "What Makes a Good Reward?" suggests following his S.M.A.R.T. format. In S.M.A.R.T. he states that rewards should be:

- **Sincere** – The reward should reflect a genuine expression of appreciation.

- **Meaningful** - to endure a motivating influence, rewards should be aligned with the values, goals, and priorities that matter the most.

- **Adaptable** - Consider creative options to keep your program fresh. No single reward format works for everyone all the time.

- **Relevant** No matter how formal or informal, expensive or affordable, the relevance of any recognition will be improved with a personal touch - it's a little thing that makes a big difference.

- **Timely** - Don't let too much time pass or the reward may be devalued and credibility eroded.

Regardless of if you use the S.M.A.R.T. format or just brainstorm with your team, having the employee recognition program clearly defined will make it easier for everyone.

Employee Involvement

Ask for your employees' thoughts about the program to make it more effective. Ask them if they consider the rewards you've selected meaningful and valuable. Involving your senior employees in the creation of the guidelines is a great avenue to take. Your senior employees have experience and can give you useful insights. Your company will be able to reach its goals if your team feels included in the program.

Get the support of both lower and upper management. Employees have a need to gain recognition from bosses. Having your management team on board can help inspire employees to utilize your program.

An alternative is to construct an employee recognition committee. Having a committee of employees and management can help you see the bigger picture. Employee participation in your program helps to ensure that the program is seen as fair. Each department should have an employee representative to serve on a committee. It is important to decide the function of the committee. The committee could be in charge of determining the parameters of the recognition program, and verifying that the policies are being upheld. The committee could also be in charge of nominating the employees.

Budget

Once you have selected the goals of your program, you will want to constitute a budget. It's important to remember that an extravagant budget is not necessarily required. Rewards can be anything from a high five to an all-expenses paid vacation. When creating a budget, make sure the rewards offered are attainable for more than just one year. You don't want to start a program, only to disassemble it the following year due to budget issues.

Talk to your management team or any department that would be in charge of allocating funds toward an employee recognition program. Decide collectively how much the company wants to spend on the program. Remember that saying, "Thank you!" is free.

Keep it Simple

Designing an employee recognition program can be likened to a snowball rolling down a hill. When the ball rolls down the hill, it collects snow. The bigger the snowball gets the more snow it collects and the faster it grows. What seems to start out small and simple can grow large and complicated very easily. When you are developing your program, make sure to keep the guidelines as clear and simple as possible. Check with your staff to see if they have questions about the program. If so, you may need to rethink some of its aspects.

- Keep the guidelines simple and clear

- Provide examples of what you expect

- Provide tools that explain the goals or criteria

- Offer training and information sessions

Practical Illustration

Johnathan is an owner of a small bakery that has been in his family for generations. He has a very small group of 15 employees. Since he has taken over the business, from his father, he has made a few changes in the bakery. The changes implemented have really helped increase the popularity of his products. Because of the influx of demand, he has streamlined some of the former processes so the bakery could produce more product. As production increased, he noticed that his employees seemed less content, and some quit their jobs. He was reminded that he needs his employees in order to make the company a success, he couldn't do it alone. He decided to ask his employees what would make them more content.

Through communication with his staff he realized they felt underappreciated and uninformed about what was going on in the company. He and a few employees formed a committee and made a list of goals and behaviors he wanted to achieve, two for the company and two personal goals for Johnathan.

- Increase productivity by 5%.
- Decrease the number of accidents in the bakery.
- Say thank you to one or more employees each day.
- Increase the amount of employee feedback and input.

Jonathan had a staff meeting to tell his employees why the changes were made, and what he wants the company to grow into. He shared his goals for the company, and shared his personal goals for himself and staff. He made sure to follow through on his personal goals, and the employees in return followed through on his company goals. His employees were very happy with these changes, and with the communication they were now receiving from their leader. The productivity increased so much that they surpassed their 5% goal, and were able to set a new one. More demand for Jonathan's baked goods, meant more employees could be hired. Soon, Johnathan had a work force of 50, all of whom were engaged in their jobs.

Personal Journal - *What are two or three points you can take from this chapter to enhance your company's employee recognition experience?*

Next to excellence is the appreciation of it.

William Makepeace Thackeray

Chapter Three:
How To Get The Buzz Out

How can an employee recognition program be effective if no one knows anything about it? Like in any relationship, communication is the key!! You have to get the buzz out about your program, get excited about it! Making the work environment more enjoyable is a big deal! You wouldn't launch a new product line without advertising would you? Don't be afraid to get out there and tell everyone the good news!

Be Creative With Designs

Look around at the products and businesses that you love, what do they have in common? The majority of them have some type of logo, engaging theme, thoughtful design, or all of the above. Let's take a moment and really take a deeper look into these three marketing tactics.

For example, think of NBC, Apple, Adidas, Chevrolet, and Yahoo. When you think of their company you think of their logos. Having a logo is a great way to connect your program with a visual image. Like logos, the design used in advertising your program can have an impact. Colors create specific subconscious emotional reactions within people. The style of font can also invoke that same kind of reaction. You will want to do some research and see what colors and font best display the type of emotion you are trying to invoke.

Another way to create a great buzz is to decide a theme. A theme is a specific ambiance or setting. Themes are great in connecting people to your program. Your theme could be simple or it could be complex. Make sure that it is something people can connect and relate to. A popular theme example would be a super hero theme. When we think of super heroes, we first think of the characters we all know – Superman, Spiderman, and Wonder Woman. We think of noble men and women who work hard and do the right thing. Attaching a theme like that to a program helps make it fun, fun that your employees will remember.

The themes do not have to be elaborate, they can be very simple. The premise is just to keep the program in the minds of your employees. If they are thinking about the program, they will most likely be participating in the program.

Paper the Walls

Logo and design have no purpose if you don't see them. A key cornerstone in advertising is print ads. Let's look at a little history.

The first full-page advertisement in the United States was placed by Robert Bonner, proprietor of the *New York Ledger*, in his rival James Gordon Bennett's *New York Herald,* on June 7, 1856. Bonner had contracted with popular novelist, Fanny Fern to provide him with a series, to be paid at the low rate of $100 a column. The advertisement for this story created such demand for the *Ledger* that its circulation nearly doubled to 50,000.

How can you apply that to your employee recognition program? Print up fliers and hang them in areas where employees congregate. If you have an employee newsletter place your own ad for the program. Hand out fliers with paychecks. Think thoughtfully about where these fliers and signs would grab your own attention, and ask employees their thoughts.

Having fliers out where people can read them is a great way to inform your employees, and get them excited.

Use Social Media

When a business wants to drum up free advertising, where do they go? Social Media! Social media is defined by Merriam-Webster Dictionary as a form of electronic communication through which users create online communities to share information, ideas, personal messages, and other content. Facebook, Twitter, Instagram, Pinterest, and YouTube are some of the most popular media sites out there today. One report showed that the majority of web surfing was on social media sites. Using social media is essentially like having a huge bullhorn to spread the word to your employees!

A recent study showed that 56% of Americans have a social media site. 23% of Americans check their Facebook more than five times a day. Americans aged 18-64 who use social networks say they spend an average of 3.2 hours per day doing so, according to new research released by Ipsos Open Thinking Exchange (OTX).

Specifically, among American social network users:

- 18-34-year-olds report spending 3.8 hours a day;

- 35-49-year-olds report spending 3 hours per day; and

- 50-64-year-olds report spending 2.4 hours per day.

Think of all that time we spend on social media. This is an amazing venue to share information with your staff. Communication through social media can also make management more personal and approachable. In recent times, even local government has jumped on the social media bandwagon.

Go Mobile!

As technology advances, so must we. In this day, over 60% of Americans own a smart phone, and that number is constantly growing. As a society we can now do almost anything from our smart phones. Ordering pizza, checking our bank account, video chatting, scanning documents, and sending grandma a birthday card can all be done with a press of a button. Many companies are designing mobile applications specifically for communications between employer and employee. Teambox is a popular new tool. It started out as a project management tool, it now has messaging capabilities also. Yammer is a good way to communicate with your company. Yammer is like Twitter, but isn't open for public viewing. The program will only let people with the company email address view the communications. On the program, you can put project updates, send messages to other employees, have groups, and form private team message boards.

Your company does not have to invest in new software, or mobile applications. The majority of smart phone users have their social media applications right on their phones. At the end of the day, it's all about communication. You have to establish what is going to be the most effective strategy to gain interest in your employee recognition program.

Practical Illustration

Herman, a blind homeless man, was sitting on a bus bench with a sign asking for change. The bench was located on a busy street, with lots of foot traffic. The sign he had was written in pencil on cardboard and just said "Blind- $ needed." He had been there for hours, and no one had stopped to give him any money. A young woman walked by him and stopped. She saw that he was completely ignored by the passing public. She decided that changing his sign would catch more attention from the public. She walked over to the man and introduced herself. She asked Herman if he minded her changing his sign. He agreed that she could change whatever she liked. She took a white shoe box lid that was sitting on the ground, and wrote with a thick black marker. The woman smiled and wished the guy luck. Almost instantly people began giving Herman money. After a while, the blind man had more money than he had ever made. Curious, he asked a young man what the sign said. "It says," said the young man, "It's a gorgeous day. You can see it. I cannot."

Personal Journal - *What are two or three points you can take from this chapter to enhance your company's employee recognition experience?*

> *Appreciation is a wonderful thing: It makes what is excellent in others belong to us as well.*
>
> *Voltaire*

Chapter Four:
It Starts From The Top!

Feeling appreciated is an important part of the workplace dynamic. A 2011 report on Employee Recognition found that only 14% of organizations provide training on recognition to managers. Part of a manager's job is to influence their employees to work hard, and work smart. Instead of just saying thank you to an employee who has been with the company for 10 years, take the time to give them some sort of certificate, or thoughtful gift. Providing well thought recognition will result in better morale and productivity.

Identifying Desirable Behaviors

The major goal of recognition is to increase the repetition of desirable behaviors. To do this, many times you have to get the employees to actually change their behavior patterns. When attempting to change an employee's behavior, you have to understand that you cannot change it for them; they have to change it themselves. A manager has to be able to identify the type of behaviors the company needs and inspire their employees to adopt those behaviors. Rewarding desired behaviors increases the repetition of the desired behaviors, and that leads to an increase in productivity.

When it comes to identifying desirable behaviors, there are no black and white guidelines. As a manager, you have to use your best judgment, but that doesn't mean you have to do it alone. Ask fellow employees what they feel are desirable behaviors in the workplace. When deciding what behaviors to reward, remember the following:

- Behavior is something the employee physically does.

- The behavior you are rewarding must be specific and easy to understand. For example, closing sales, calculating cash receipts, etc.

- The behavior you are rewarding must be easy to measure accurately.

Behaviors are different from skills, habits, and talents. A behavior is something the employee can influence and control, attitudes, and feelings aren't behavior.

Understanding the Goals of the Company

There is an old saying, *"If you don't know where you came from, how can you know where you're going?"* If you don't know your company policies and goals, how can you hope to help reach and surpass them? When implementing an employee recognition program, you will need to identify the behavior you want to reward, as we just covered. To aid in this, you need to know what the goals of your company are. Talking with your upper management team and asking questions is a good way to start this process. Do research on the goal you want to set. On performance based recognition, you will want to obtain reports on what the current status is, and talk to professionals on what a reasonable goal would be. Talking to professionals, management, and researching the goal you want to set will help you to make sure the goal is attainable and fair. Take the time to read the policies, and make sure that you have complete understanding of them.

Setting Guidelines

According to Webster's dictionary, guideline is defined as a general rule, principle, or piece of advice. A guideline is a statement by which to determine a course of action. A guideline aims to streamline particular processes according to a set routine or sound practice.

We have discussed prior, that making sure you're guidelines are clear and simple is imperative for success. Training management on how to draft those guidelines is paramount. Keep in mind that a good recognition and reward system provides employees with three things:

- A reasonable reward for their efforts

- Inspiration to sustain and improve their job performance

- A clear description of what behaviors the company values

When setting guidelines, make sure that you follow within the parameters of your company policies and goals.

Providing Recognition Templates

Employee recognition tools and templates should be provided for supervisors and coworkers to use to recognize and reward employees and teams. A template for recognition can increase the regularity of its practice. A great idea for on the spot recognition would be providing managers with company cards. An online feedback system could allow managers or co-workers to submit recognition for a job well. Template rewards are not the only rewards that should be used, but it will help maintain the frequency of the praise.

Practical Illustration

Samuel has worked at his company for 10 years. He started as a janitor, and worked his way up the ladder. He has recently been promoted to a management position. He wants to make a real difference in his company. The company has provided him with all of the training he could ever need on the technical aspects of his position, but little to no training on recognition. Samuel speaks to his manager, and asks if there are any opportunities to gain training on employee recognition. Soon after, he and his boss have an informal training session with human resources. Samuel starts his preparation for launching an employee recognition program with his supervisor's blessing.

Personal Journal - *What are two or three points you can take from this chapter to enhance your company's employee recognition experience?*

If you're not shown appreciation, it gets to you.

Kareem Abdul-Jabbar

Chapter Five:
Creating a Culture of Recognition

According to Dr. Bob Nelson, employees in a company that has a culture of recognition are 5 times more likely to feel valued, 7 times more likely to stay, and 11 times more likely to feel completely committed to their jobs and mission of the organization.

Fun Facts about Employee Recognition from You earned it:

- Happy employees are 85% more efficient

- Happy employees are 55% more effective

- Happy employees deliver 42% better customer service

- Happy employees stick around 2x longer than unhappy employees

- 80% of Gen Y said they prefer on-the-spot recognition over formal reviews, and feel that this is imperative for their growth and understanding of a job.

Keep Your Staff "In the Know"

Communication is the key to success in ANY relationship. Engagement and motivation are cultivated, they don't manifest by themselves. Employees thrive on information and communication flowing freely back and forth between you and them. Your employees want to know what is going on with the company.

1) **Have meetings!** According to a survey done by Employment Review, holding a meeting is the most effective way you can keep your employees informed about existing organizational issues.

2) **Email updates about company projects.** The same survey done by Employment Review has pointed out e-mail updates as the second most popular communication method among organizations.

3) **Create a company newsletter.** Email should not be your only form of communication with your company. Giving your employees access to the latest company news can help keep them engaged.

According to a study done by Forbes, companies that scored in the top 20% for building a culture of recognition enjoyed a 31% lower voluntary turnover rate.

Empower Employees with Peer to Peer Recognition

Why should you implement a peer-to-peer recognition program? Peer to peer recognition programs have many benefits. They are relatively easy to institute, and don't require a lot of money. These programs can connect large groups of employees. It is very nice to be recognized by your supervisor, but having the recognition of your co-workers is equally important. A peer to peer program can make the employee getting praise feel good, as well as the one giving the praise. Employees have more exchanges with their peers than with management. Peer recognition can significantly boost an employee's self-esteem. Having a system that allows employees to receive numerous types of recognition enriches your program. You can support your peer recognition program by:

- Provide recognition and rewards for participation.
- Send recognition to an individual in person.
- Send flowers.

- Set up a nomination system that recognizes the efforts of employees who improve the workplace.
- Invite employees into your office to thank them personally.
- Express interest in your employees' professional development.

It can't be overstated how much your employees are at the heart of your business.

Team Building: Encourage Camaraderie

What is a team? According to Webster's dictionary, a team is a group of employees who unite around a particular task or objective. A team is a way of organizing different people with different goals and plans into a cohesive whole. When a team is successful, it focuses the energy of team members for the good of the organization.

A team effort almost always outweighs an individual effort. Most often teams are more productive. Sometimes though, groups can have obstacles. Disagreements can be a big issue when working in a team setting. Communication with team members is the only way to dissipate these hindrances. When workers get to know one another and are comfortable around each other, teamwork can be heightened. Camaraderie can be achieved by participating in activities. These activities can be as simple as grabbing a snack together, or a more elaborate like going on a team building retreat.

The environment you work in is changing and growing so rapidly that it is impossible to meet the challenges alone. You have to rely on the other members of your teams.

Motivate by Promoting Fun

According to Baudville.com, in a given year, we spend nearly 2,300 hours at work. That is a lot of time! Add some fun to your working hours to help increase morale. Challenge yourself to continually generate fun and positive energy. Achieving this task will affect not only you, but your employees around you, creating a more productive workplace.

Be organized to get energized, surround yourself with things that bring joy. Encourage employees to decorate their workspaces with things that have meaning in their life, or add fun such as:

- Photographs in fun frames.
- Potted plants in creative containers.
- Personalized sticky notes.
- Colored file folders.

- Colored paper clips, creative post-its.
- A fun calendar.

There are a few simple guidelines to remember when trying to add some fun into your workplace. You want the employees to have a good time but not offend anyone.

Workplace fun should:

- Be appropriate for the workplace
- Involve as many employees as possible
- Be sensitive to how people might react

Workplace fun should not:

- Sexist or vulgar
- Offend anyone
- Make fun of anyone
- Be sarcastic
- Detract from core business
- Damage the reputation of individuals
- Damage the reputation of the company

Champion the cause for creating an enjoyable workplace. Combine fun and effectiveness by timing yourself while working. See if you can beat your best time, or challenge a coworker. Make your workplace fun and ask your staff what would make their jobs more enjoyable. Employees that play together stay together.

Practical Illustration

To Darren, an employee-of-the-month program seemed like the least time-consuming way to make sure his staff felt appreciated as his business grew. Imagine his surprise to find out his program wasn't helping morale. Based on information gained from employees during informal conversations, he realized a less rigid, more personal approach was in order. He encouraged his management team to get in the habit of reporting employee positive efforts. He set aside part of his daily scheduled phones call with executives to discuss exemplary work, in addition to 15 minutes in of each weekly meeting. Darren also made an effort to thank employees often with handwritten notes mailed to their homes. Stephanie, an employee of three years, was pleasantly surprised to find a note from Darren in her mailbox. In the note, handwritten on company stationery, Darren noted that Stephanie had been praised during several recent management meetings for working closely with a customer and thanked her for her hard work. Stephanie told Darren the personal and unique note made her feel important, especially since she was sure Darren had a million other things to do during the day.

Personal Journal - *What are two or three points you can take from this chapter to enhance your company's employee recognition experience?*

Of all of our inventions for mass communication, pictures still speak the most universally understood language.

Walt Disney

Chapter Six:
The Best Things In Life Are Free!

Tough economic times don't mean that you can't recognize your employees. There are so many ways that you can reward employees without writing a check. A survey found that "frequent of accomplishments" was the top non-monetary compensation named by employees with "regular communication" coming in at No. 2. Both activities can make your staff more productive without shaving one millimeter off your bottom line.

Put a Spotlight on Employees in Staff Meetings

Good communication between management and employees is the cornerstone of a well-run company. Poor communication between management and employees can be a source of concern and lost productivity. You may see each of your employees daily, but if you don't have regular, ongoing communication with employees as a group, those relationships will not live up to their potential. All employees want to feel that they have something important to offer the company. The team atmosphere can be increased through employee meetings. At employee meetings, you provide the big picture. Employees interact with their managers daily regarding specific tasks. However, they may not be exposed to the goals and progress of company. An employee meeting provides an arena for sharing this information. The employee meeting is the perfect audience to give praise to some of your staff members. Sharing praise publicly can boost the morale of your employees.

The employee getting praised is uplifted, and the employees around them can use their example. There are a few ways to boost your employee or employees' in the meeting. Here are some examples:

- Single out an individual, discuss what they did that was positive and how it affected the company.

- Prepare a presentation that celebrates the employee's accomplishments.

- Recognize a group or department as a whole. Discuss their achievements.

Write it Down

Personal, handwritten notes grow rarer day by day. According to the U.S. Postal Service's annual survey, the average home only received a personal letter once every seven weeks in 2010, down from once every two weeks in 1987. We live in a strange world where emails and text messages are more popular than handwritten notes. These days, who has time for stamps, stationery, and where's the spell-check? A recent study from The Radicati Group indicated the average corporate email account sent or received more than 100 emails per day, and Americans between the ages of 18 and 29 now send or receive nearly 100 texts per day. Emails, tweets, texts, or Facebook messages are fairly effortless. Handwritten notes are unique because they are a rarity and unusual. They take minutes (or hours) to write, and do not have an "undo" button. Drafting a letter involves picking out stationery, paying for stamps, and going to a mailbox. They are an investment in time and effort.

If, as the U.S. Postal Service notes, we only receive a handwritten letter once every two months, each of those letters likely means more to us than the "cheaper" communication we receive each day. While saying "thank you" is great, a well-crafted handwritten note can show an investment and appreciation that a simple thank-you can't. In a world where communication is so accessible, these simple acts of gratitude, and appreciation can show the people who matter to your business that they are important to you. Handwritten letters provide a sense of nostalgia. They let your employees know you appreciate them enough to take 15 minutes to put pen to paper in an attempt to connect with them. Here are some ideas on the types of handwritten notes your employees may appreciate:

- A handwritten thank you note.

- Write a note to their family, telling them how important the employee's efforts have been to the company.

- Provide them with a formal letter of appreciation for their file.

- Get each employee to write something positive about the person on a piece of paper, and give them the box of collected sayings, or frame them for the employee.

Display Your Appreciation

It may seem like an unimportant issue, but allowing employees to display awards will work out to your advantage. A wall of fame lets your employees show their recognition, but are not permitted to display it, you lose part of the benefit of your recognition program. What are the benefits to the company of providing employee recognition awards and allowing them to be displayed?

The first asset is that seeing the commendation daily reinforces the kind of performance that is valued by the company. No matter what the award is for, the employee who sees their award daily will recollect the joy of being recognized as a valued member of the company.

The second asset of having commendations displayed is to increase productivity and quality of work for all employees. Employees will want to obtain employee recognition awards. Those employees will work harder to produce the kind of work that earned the award. Everyone wants to be recognized for their work. The incentive helps produce better work in greater quantities in order to achieve success. Here are a few ideas for your employee wall of recognition:

- Have an employee of the month or year with a photo.

- Have a wall of fame, where employee achievements are put.

- Have an area in the employee's office or cubical where they can individually display their awards.

Make Work More Comfortable

In general, employers find that their employees who are content in the work place tend to be more productive. A comfortable work environment is crucial to getting positive results out of your employees. It is fairly easy to add comfort into your recognition program. How can you reward with comfort in mind? Here are some ideas:

- Casual (clothes) Day
- Let the employee assign to you the one project they like least.
- A reserved parking spot.
- A vacation day.
- Create a certificate that they can submit to take any day off, no questions asked.
- Allow them to have flexible hours.
- Allow them choose one day a week to work from home.

- Have a potluck lunch, everyone brings a dish! This is of no cost to the company and allows employees to get together.
- Wacky Pajama Day. Allow employees to wear pajamas and slippers to work for maximum comfort.

It is important for employers to remember at all times that employees are likely to spend more time at work than anywhere else. Having your employees comfortable in their work environment and happy will bring your company success.

Practical Illustration

Ella is a hard working employee. She has helped thousands of customers and truly enjoys her job. Recently the management team in her company has changed, and they have begun implementing some employee recognition tactics that makes Ella feel appreciated. The company has started having employee social gatherings, like potluck lunches. She has had a chance to get to know, and enjoy the company, of her fellow co-workers. The company has also implemented a casual Friday where she can wear jeans to work. The new management team has also implemented a wall of fame. Ella is very excited by the prospect of qualifying for employee of the month. All of the rewards that the company has implemented cost nothing, but have impacted greatly.

Personal Journal - *What are two or three points you can take from this chapter to enhance your company's employee recognition experience?*

It has long been an axiom of mine that the little things are infinitely the most important.

Arthur Conan Doyle

Chapter Seven:
A Small Gesture Goes A Long Way

Employees are the heart of any business. Employees who are not engaged can drain the positive energy out of the office atmosphere. Enthusiasm is infectious, and employees who are engaged spread their enthusiasm to not only employees but customers. Happy employees are the biggest gain to any business' bottom line. Keeping your employees engaged in their job does not have to break the bank. We will explore how to recognize your employees while staying in a budget.

Have a Party!

Supervisors who have a positive relationship with their employees are more likely to have an engaged staff. Staff appreciation functions provide the opportunity for employees to connect with their co-workers and supervisors. We have all heard the expressions "you catch more flies with honey" and "a way to a man's heart is through his stomach". Having a party or some sort of treat is an easy and inexpensive way to show your appreciation.

Here are some party ideas:

- Ice cream party.
- Bring doughnuts for the staff.
- Have a popcorn break.
- Invite their spouse in for a lunch, company's treat.
- Have a hero sandwich party for your superhero staff.
- Once a year, have a day where you appreciate your staff. Have management cook and serve food.
- Provide a lunch on a busy day or during a project.
- Throw a pizza lunch party.
- Write "Thank you. You are a _____!" on a roll of Lifesavers.
- Serve lemonade for a refreshing break.

Even if you just put on music and give them a cookie, the employees you recognize will be ecstatic that their work was noticed and appreciated.

Make a Game of It

A psychologist recently wrote in an article for The Capital, that "only 29% of employees in a typical company are actively engaged in their job." Keeping your employees engaged does not have to bankrupt the company. Workplace interactions that are positive are an integral part of any professional relationship. Regardless of if you are interacting with a peer, supervisor, or customer, effective communication is always necessary. Employee recognition programs that utilize a game will help dissipate frustration in the office, and keep your employees engaged.

Ideas for employee recognition games:

- Create a poster for each staff member that has positive attributes for each letter in his or her name. For example: Tripp=Timely, Rational, Innovative, Passionate, and Professional.
- Have a raffle. Award employees with tickets, and have a weekly or monthly drawing for a prize.
- "Wheel of Recognition" – Select 3 stellar employees to spin the wheel for a reward.

Fun appreciation games aid in improving communication and motivation among co-workers. This creates a more productive work environment.

Reward with Small Gift

Feeling appreciated is one of the biggest

arguments for employee recognition programs. As we have said before, and can't say enough, it doesn't have to cost you a lot of money or time!

- Award problem solvers with a puzzle.
- New office furniture like a desk or a chair.
- Pay for them to take a fun class, such as painting or wine tasting.
- Find something they like to collect, such as baseball cards, and add to their collection.
- Give them a gift card for their favorite stores.
- Buy a book for them, by an author they like.
- Buy a CD for them, by an artist they like.
- Give them movie tickets for the family.
- Give them a gas card to help out with gas prices.
- Have a birthday cake for their birthday.
- Pay for a subscription to their favorite magazine.
- Stop by a dollar store and pick up a bunch of small gifts to use for on-the-spot recognition.

With so many ways to recognize employees while staying on budget, there's no reason not to reward your employees for positive behavior. As an employer, you can develop a happy and productive workplace environment by recognizing your employees whenever applicable.

Give Them a Break

Employee recognition programs can stimulate performance, and impact your company profits. Most of us work 40 hours or more a week, that can add up to over 2000 hours a year!! We spend so much time at work; sometimes it's nice to have a break. Here are some ideas to help:

- Have a nap time
- 30 minutes TV break
- 15 minute Facebook break
- Longer lunch break
- Keep food or drinks in the break room for employees to enjoy
- PTO (paid time off)
- Let them leave early one day (with pay)
- Pass around Kit-Kat bars at break time, singing the "give me a break" song

Practical Illustration

James is struggling to engage his employees. He tells them on a constant basis that he appreciates them but he wants to do more. He went to his supervisor to discuss getting funding for an employee recognition program. His supervisor approved the program but said the company could only spend $30 a month on the program. James brainstormed with his employees and decided that he would throw a movie party. He brought a movie from home, gathered his team in the conference room where there is a large TV. During the movie he serves iced tea he made, and popcorn. The next month he decides to change it up and have a sundae party. His employees look forward to the monthly celebration and morale is higher than ever.

Personal Journal - *What are two or three points you can take from this chapter to enhance your company's employee recognition experience?*

People are definitely a company's greatest asset. It doesn't make any difference whether the product is cars or cosmetics. A company is only as good as the people it keeps.

Mary Kay Ash

Chapter Eight:
Pulling Out The Red Carpets

Giving recognition to all of your employees is critical. When striving for excellence, sometimes you have to spend money. Having a reward that people really want to work for can benefit your company more than the cost of the reward.

According to Awardco, "MGM documented their 2005 recognition program, tracking individual productivity in each department, employee satisfaction surveys, and employee turnover. MGM noted that employee satisfaction rose to 90.3%, turnover dropped to 11.4%, and revenues rose from $714 million to more than $1 billion."

Have an Awards Ceremony

Sometimes a small party in the break room just isn't enough to tell your staff how much you appreciate what they do on a daily basis. Having a lavish party or awards ceremony can really show them that they are important to you and your company. Most don't get to go to an awards banquet very often, so having something in their honor is exciting.

To make it special, use some sort of theme. A great recognition event can create or increase pride, employee satisfaction, and trust.

According to Chester Elton and Adrian Gostick, authors of *Managing with Carrots*, *The 24 Carrot Manager* and *A Carrot A Day*, "The world's most successful organizations have learned that they must make a recognition event something memorable - with almost as much ceremony and emotion as an Olympic-medal event."

Here are some pointers to make your event great:

- Send invitations in the mail- this makes the event feel more important and special.
- Choose theme- the theme can be as simple as *Super customer service* or *the golden globes*, but make sure it is something that your staff members can connect with.
- Choose the awards and determine what the award should symbolize.
- Notify presenters personally.
- Notify award winners personally.

Win Large Items

Having an incentive that really excites employees is important. Sometimes the $10 gift card isn't enough for them to want to really push the envelope and go above and beyond the call of duty. Being able to offer a reward that really drives an employee is a huge bonus. These large items can be offered to a group as a whole or to an individual. When deciding to offer a larger item, just make sure that it fits the task at hand, and that the regulations are fair. Here are a few ideas for larger ticket items as rewards.

Individual:

- Win a TV
- Win a monetary bonus
- Win a car
- Win a new kitchen

Group Rewards:

- Have a massage therapist come to the office give a massages to the staff
- Have a family portrait session. Pay for employees to have their family photos taken
- Have a mobile car wash come to the company and clean employees cars

GoDaddy sets money aside every month that is used to take employees off-site for activities during paid work hours. Recent GoDaddy expeditions include: whitewater rafting, gold panning, cooking classes, and trapeze classes.

Vacation

It's easy to view an absent employee as an unfavorable commodity for a company. Studies have shown that never taking time off can produce a large amount of issues, from health problems to mental burnout. Everyone needs a vacation once in a while. A regular employee may not experience the kind of stressors the company president has, but all of us has job-related stress. We may face the anxiety of meeting deadlines, making important decisions, or taxing physical demands. Everyone has some form of stress in their life, even if they don't acknowledge it.

Constant stress takes its toll on our body's ability to fight off infection, maintain homeostasis, and avoid injuries. When you're stressed out and tired, you are more likely to contract illnesses, you can develop heart issues, and you are more likely to have injuries. A recent study showed that failing to take vacations could increase your risk of heart disease by up to 30 percent. In *Success under*

Stress, author Sharon Melnick writes that 80% of workers feel stress on the job, and 70% of healthcare provider visits are due to stress-related conditions. Stress can cause insomnia, high blood pressure, and a wealth of other health issues. Stress can affect you physically and also mentally. Stress can make you become depressed, cause anxiety, and irritable. Your memory will suffer as well, and could lead to you making poor decisions. Fatigue and stress decrease your motor and mental functions, which could result in a drop in productivity.

Vacations help employees alleviate excess stress. Generally, when an employee returns from vacation, they are ready to tackle the world again. Breaks exist to give us the opportunity to recharge ourselves. We all need a break sometimes both physically and mentally. Here are some suggestions on how to turn a needed vacation into a reward:

- Award three-day cruise tickets for a short vacation.
- Award them with an all-expenses paid camping trip.
- Award them with a trip to a major city like New York or Las Vegas.

- Award them with a trip to a city known for its fabulous shopping areas!

A rested mind is an efficient mind. Workers who refuse to take vacations every now and again become weighed down in the stress of life.

Career Advancement

The whole point of an employee recognition program is to recognize those employees who do excellent work, and keep them. Most employees do not want to stay in the same position for their whole life. Giving them a chance to advance is the best way to keep them at the company, happy and engaged.

Offering a promotion to deserving employees is a big motivator. An employee's hard work should be rewarded. Not all employees can qualify on their own for a higher ranking job, though. Sometimes an additional certificate or degree is necessary. Offering a reimbursement program for college classes is a good step in career advancement. As an employee, personal growth is crucial. Having company support makes the employee feel valued. Education can benefit the employee and the company. The employee gets further or new training to help in their position, or help qualify them for another position. The company now can offer positions in-house to employees, whereas before they would have had to pay for training and new employee costs.

Intel offers $50,000 for tuition reimbursement and an eight-week paid sabbatical every seven years, which 4067 employees took advantage of in 2012.

Practical Illustration

Two companies, Texas Apple Orchards and Sweet Apple Cider, wanted to combine their companies into one, called Sweet Texas Co. They created a task force with members from each company to make the transition as smooth as possible. The task force was assigned with informing the employees of the policy changes, and outlining the policies and job duties. The task force worked for 6 months, working sometimes 60 hour weeks and weekends to make sure the transition went off without a hitch. On the day the two companies became one, the task force's hard work had finally paid off. The two companies' employees understood their new roles, and were excited about the changes. The new CEO presented them with a handwritten note granting them a much needed two week vacation. The company even gave the employees their choice of vacation destination. The task force employees were so thankful to have the time off to rejuvenate and for having a great company to come back to.

Personal Journal - *What are two or three points you can take from this chapter to enhance your company's employee recognition experience?*

> *Make it a habit to tell people thank you. To express your appreciation, sincerely and without the expectation of anything in return. Truly appreciate those around you, and you'll soon find many others around you. Truly appreciate life, and you'll find that you have more of it.*
>
> **Ralph Marston**

Chapter Nine:
The Don'ts of Employee Recognition

Most employers are aware of the benefits of employee recognition programs. These programs can aid in increased productivity, a happier staff, a loyal staff, lower job abandonment, and decrease absenteeism. Many businesses still have not appointed an employee recognition program, or they have and program is failing. Why would an employee recognition program fail? The following are some major employee recognition "don'ts."

Don't Forget About The Art Of The High Five!

Recognition makes an employee feel like they are Rocky when he finishes climbing the Philadelphia Museum of Art stairs. I think we can all say that we have been at work and wanted someone to recognize how awesome we are. Something as simple as a high five, or a hand shake can make you feel great. Management should show their employees as often as possible that they are appreciated. It doesn't always have to be a formal ceremony or a plaque, just a high five and "you're doing great" is enough sometimes. According to International Association of Business Communicators, research shows that the most meaningful type of feedback is a heartfelt "great job" that comes from someone the employee respects. Having praise from a respected member of management is a boost that is free.

Here are some examples to informally recognize an employee:

- Call the employee into your office to say thank you for a job well done.
- Give high fives
- Post-it Thank you notes
- Greet employees by name
- Practice behaviors that show your appreciation, like giving your employee a sincere smile or a handshake

Having an attitude of gratitude is infectious, so watch out!

Don't Let It Become Boring

For everyone there is that one commercial on TV that you roll your eyes when it comes on. It seems that is the only commercial the station has to play sometimes. You are so bored with watching it, you turn off the TV.

Companies are busy and ever changing places. New policies and projects are created and completed daily. Priorities can change quickly when people are busy. An employee recognition program can easily go by the wayside. The trick is to keep the program in the minds of both staff and management. The marketing for the program must be just as compelling as the program. You will want to consider, what is the best type of marketing to make your program stand out? You want to also determine the right time to dazzle your audience with information about the program. For example, telling employees about the program when they are stressed out and busy is probably not going to be as effective. Having a meeting after projects have slowed down may be the more effective route to go. Take the time to talk to you staff and see what they need, or want for the program.

Popularity Contest or Recognition Program?

Are you running a popularity contest or an employee recognition program? Your intention when creating the program is to recognize stellar employees. When a voting system comes into play you can sometimes run into the dreaded popularity contest. Popularity should have nothing to do with employee recognition. If an employee does exemplary work than they should be recognized, seems simple, right? When your employee recognition program seems like a popularity contest, the employees see it as favoritism. You can make sure this doesn't happen by being very clear about the eligibility and judging parameters. Be transparent about how the nominees and award winners are selected. If you form a committee that has an equal demographic slice of your company, it will seem fairer to the employees. The committee should be made up of everyone from senior management to the mail room clerk. Make sure that ever faction of your company is represented in some way. Eventually, every employee needs to be praised for something. You don't want the employees to feel like they are better or less than the others. Rewarding a select group of people will only breed conflict among your team.

Recognition opportunities should be available for all employees. Employee recognition is a powerful ally in a company. When an employee recognition program is done well, it increases morale and motivates employees. That being said, ineffective recognition efforts can cause long-lasting negativity.

Make Sure the Prize is Motivational

Motivation is the reason one has for acting or behaving in a particular way. Incentive programs fail when the reward isn't actually motivational. The best way to ensure that your program motivates all employees equally, is to give your employees choice. Poll your employees and see what rewards they would like to receive. Have different options for them to choose from. Having a system that allows employees the option to choose different prizes is a great way to keep them engaged. Think back to when you were a kid going to an arcade that gives you tickets to choose your prizes. It was exciting, as you gained tickets, you could get multiple smaller prizes or one big prize. When an employee can see a reward that they would like to receive, they will usually work even harder.

Practical Illustration

Peter works at a local fast food restaurant, and he is not particularly engaged in his job. Peter shows up late, asks to leave early and calls in more often than not. When Peter shows up for work, he usually is at least partially out of uniform and has a bad attitude. Typically during his shift, Peter will take food without paying for it and eat it in the back of the building. Management is frustrated with Peter's performance, but he is not the only employee who is not engaged in his position. The restaurant decides to start an employee of the month program. The program involves having their picture hanging up for a month, their name on a plaque, and 5 movie tickets. Peter is very interested in the movie tickets, and starts actively trying to better his work performance. After 4 months of hard work, Peter has finally gotten employee of the month. He hopes that he can achieve this accomplishment again. He is engaged and enjoying his job, and is now striving to become a shift leader.

Personal Journal - *What are two or three points you can take from this chapter to enhance your company's employee recognition experience?*

> *A genuine leader is not a searcher for consensus but a molder of consensus.*
>
> **Dr. Martin Luther King, Jr.**

Chapter Ten:
Maintaining Employee Recognition Programs

One of the greatest challenges any recognition program faces is maintaining momentum after the new wears off. Decades of studies have proven that people function better in environments that are based on rewarding employees rather than chastising them. Creating and maintaining an employee recognition program is not always a simple task. With the help of a few basic guidelines, maintaining an effective recognition program can be simple.

Change the Membership

We have talked a lot about keeping a diverse committee. Changing the committee members helps keep the program fresh. Having new eyes look at what should be rewarded, and what rewards are given can add a renewed sense of excitement and fairness. How should you begin to change the membership of the committee?

- Include former award recipients

- Include all staff levels and representation from all areas of the organization

- Be transparent about your selection process

Include In New Employee Orientation

Employee recognition is not a common element of many workplaces according to HR.com who did a study showing that less than 20% indicated they are recognized monthly or more often. Don't assume that new employees coming into the company know how to use the program. You will want to have some sort of information so that they know what you expect them to achieve.

Training new employees on recognition also means training them on how to give effective peer to peer recognition. Train your new employees to recognize others. Share with them who is receiving recognition and what they did to receive it. Give examples of what is appropriate recognition, and make sure they understand the criteria. Provide them with what you consider the best types of encouragement that they can give coworkers. Encourage regular, visible support and participation from senior management.

Keep Marketing!

Organizations invest a lot in employee recognition, spending on average 1% of the payroll on recognition activities. A survey by HR.com showed that 73% of HR representatives reported that their organizations have an employee recognition program in place. 58% of those companies' employees reported that their organization does not have an employee recognition program. This shows us that despite the investment that a company provides for an employee recognition program, many employees do not even know those programs exist. Keeping the buzz about your program going is imperative. You can start a program, but if you don't keep reminding your employees about it, they are likely to forget! Periodically, send fun reminders to all employees. Utilize your employee resources to keep them "In the know".

- Web
- Email
- Paper mail
- Newsletter
- Bulletin board
- Announce recognition when it happens

- At a meeting

Annual Awards Ceremonies

Nearly 70% of employees say they are not recognized annually. Annual awards ceremonies should be a main event in the year. An annual awards ceremony is a great annual reminder that your company rewards good work. It's important to remember to change the awards ceremony to keep it interesting. A good way to change it up would be to have a different department of your organization host the annual ceremony each year. The department can create their own unique event.

Practical Illustration

To improve its recognition efforts, the Mike's Company created a new program. Before creating the program, the Mike's Company did two things. First, it involved the company's top leaders in the recognition strategy. The company's president supports and promotes the program regularly. Second, the company established goals that would be measured after the program was implemented. Today, the Mike's Company includes a platform that allows for all employees to receive recognition. The program criteria include behaviors aligned to the company's values, providing superior service to colleagues or customers, performance, and tenure anniversaries. The company's leaders can now analyze the program successes. Meetings are held to review program usage, positive and negative attributes. To date, the Mike's Company has achieved the results it had set out to achieve prior to the program's implementation. The management team is better able to assess employee performance, in order to recognize outstanding behaviors. The company continues to set new goals for its program. They have a large variety of meaningful rewards that the employees work hard to receive.

Personal Journal - *What are two or three points you can take from this chapter to enhance your company's employee recognition experience?*

> *Everyone wants to be appreciated, so if you appreciate someone, don't keep it a secret.*
>
> **Mary Kay Ash**

Closing Thoughts

Lawrence Bossidy: I am convinced that nothing we do is more important than hiring and developing people. At the end of the day you bet on people, not on strategies.

Richard Kovacevich: When people aren't having fun, when they're not recognized for outstanding performance, when no one says 'thanks,' they do become disengaged and feel unimportant,"

Gilbert Chavez: The payoff of recognition is simple—engagement.

Dalai Lama: When you practice gratefulness, there is a sense of respect toward others.

Dan Miller: "If you want to know my identity, don't ask me what I do or where I work, rather ask me what I am doing to make my life meaningful or how I'm fulfilling my purpose in life."

Anonymous: "If you work hard at your job you can make a living, but if you work hard on yourself you can make a fortune."

Dale Carnegie: "Many people think that if they were only in some other place, or had some other job, they would be happy. Well, that is doubtful. So get as much happiness out of what you are doing as you can and don't put off being happy until some future date.".

E.M. Foster: "We must be willing to let go of the life we have planned, so as to have the life that is waiting for us."

Additional Titles Available

At thousands of major online and offline bookstores and retailers worldwide.

Visit

www.thekisstheory.com

To your continued success!

About the Author

The experience Jayne Finn, has goes back three decades, and involves training, coaching, and teaching. Jayne Finn, is a Certified Facilitator, Adjunct Instructor, and Entrepreneur. She's worked as a facilitator and consultant with various organizations including start-ups, community colleges and Fortune 100 and 500 companies. She is an advocate of lifelong learning. In her free time, Jayne enjoys long walks on the beach, collecting sea shells and photography. She graduated from North Carolina Wesleyan College with a degree in Accounting and holds Six Sigma Black Belt Certification.

With gratitude and appreciation.

www.ingramcontent.com/pod-product-compliance
Lightning Source LLC
Chambersburg PA
CBHW051335170526
45166CB00002B/828